FOUNDATIONS OF TAPPING

Inviting EFT and Other Tapping Practices into Your Life

COMPANION WORKBOOK

STACEY WEBB

Copyright © 2023 by Stacey Webb

First published in Australia in 2023 by Stacey Webb
All rights reserved. No part of this book may be reproduced by any mechanical, photographic, or electronic process, or in the form of phonographic recording; nor may it be stored in a retrieval system, transmitted, or otherwise be copied for public or private use - other than for "fair use" as brief quotations embodied in articles and reviews – without prior written permission from the publisher.

The author of this book does not dispense medical advice or prescribe the use of any technique as a form of treatment for physical, emotional, or medical problems without the advice of a physician, either directly or indirectly. The intent of the author is only to offer information of a general nature to help you in your quest for emotional and spiritual well-being. In the event you use any of the information in this book for yourself, the author and publisher assume no responsibility for your actions.

Because of the dynamic nature of the Internet, any web addresses or links contained in this book may have changed since publication and may no longer be valid.

Cover design by Ida Jensson
Edited by Dannielle Line
All images by Rachael Cannard

Foundations of Tapping/Stacey Webb

ISBN: 978-0-6458119-2-6

(Paperback)

ISBN: 978-0-6458119-3-3

(Ebook)

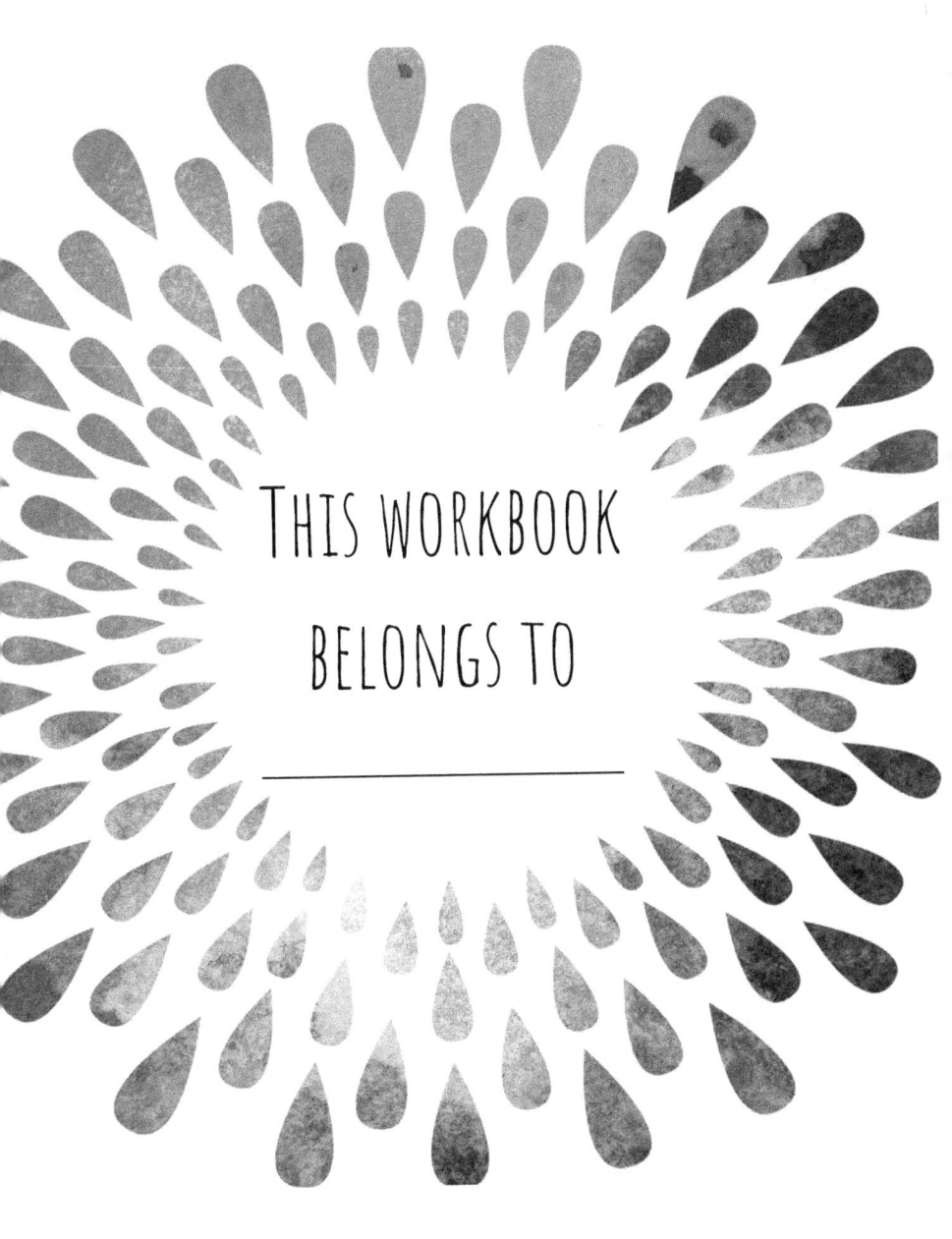

I dedicate this book to you, dear reader. For picking up this companion workbook with curiosity and willingness as you walk the path of your healing journey. It is my privilege to take this journey with you.

Acknowledgment of Country

As I explore the divine lands of Colomatta and its surroundings, I feel its expansive nature. In those moments and in every moment in between I acknowledge the Dharug and Gundungurra people of the Ngurra Nation as the infinite custodians of this place. I acknowledge your custodial care has been integral to the wonderful expression of this magical place. I see that the nurturing, care and healing you provide to this land flows back to the people through the elements of this place. I stand and witness the deep and sacred spiritual connection you have to all those elements of this Country. I pay deep respects to the Elders with much gratitude for the powerful way they lead the community. I am committed to being an ally to the Aboriginal community and supporting Aboriginal-led movements toward an equitable society.

Author Note

Emotional Freedom Techniques are still considered experimental in nature. Although it is gaining scientific support; it is not yet widely accepted as a formally validated scientific technique. It is important you take full responsibility for your own health. The content provided in this workbook is not a substitute for traditional medical attention, counselling, therapy, or advice from a qualified healthcare practitioner. It is not intended to be used to treat, diagnose, cure, or prevent any disease or disorder.

Contents

Welcome		VI
1.	The Foundations	1
2.	The Basic Recipe	7
3.	Tapping Through the Layers	25
4.	Personal Peace Procedure	57
5.	Chakra Tapping	75
6.	Other Tapping Practices	95
7.	Inviting Tapping into Your Life	101
8.	Tapping Scripts	227
9.	Reflection and Notes	233
Thank You		240
About the Author		241

Welcome

Welcome, my friends, to the Foundations of Tapping Companion Workbook.

My name is Stacey Webb. I am an Intuitive Somatic Mentor, Trauma-Trained Somatic Practitioner, EFT Practitioner, a Warrior of Grace, and a Multi-Award-Winning Author. I am excited to share this space with you.

I created this companion workbook to empower you in your own transformation. To have this tool in your hands to help you let go of the things holding you back.

How this book and the Foundations of Tapping: Inviting EFT and Other Tapping Practices into Your Life work together.

This book has an accompanying book called Foundations of Tapping: Inviting EFT and Other Tapping Practices into Your Life. I highly recommend having both books together as you work through either book. The Foundations of Tapping: Inviting EFT and Other Tapping Practices into Your Life book contains the basic history, philosophy, and principles of Emotional Freedom Techniques and other tapping practices. Reading that book will allow you to take part in the practices within this book to support your healing journey. To ensure a smooth transition between them, the chapters in both books are the same.

Allow yourself to flow through this workbook at a pace that feels comfortable for you. Give yourself permission to interact, join in the practices, and integrate the learnings.

What you learn might surprise you.

BEGINNING OF WORKBOOK

Invite yourself time to answer these questions with honesty to yourself

My reasons for wanting to use this workbook and bring tapping into my life are?

_____
_____
_____
_____
_____
_____
_____

What resistance, if any, do I have surrounding tapping?

_____
_____
_____
_____
_____
_____
_____

Chapter One

The Foundations

THE TAPPING POINTS

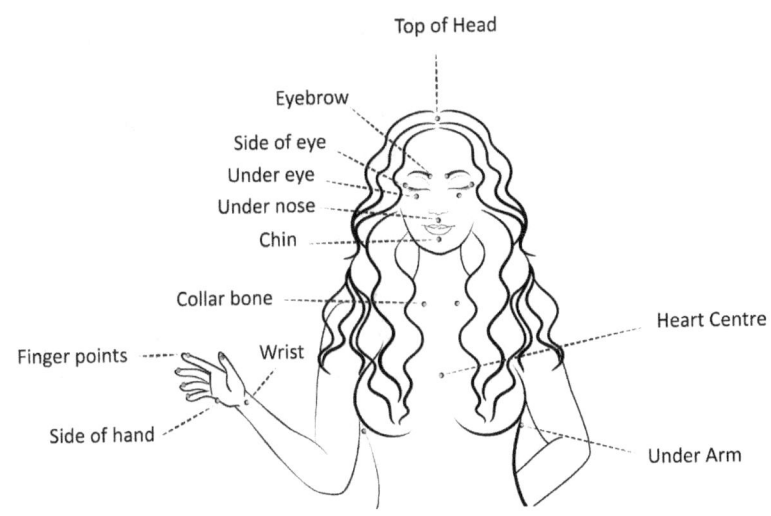

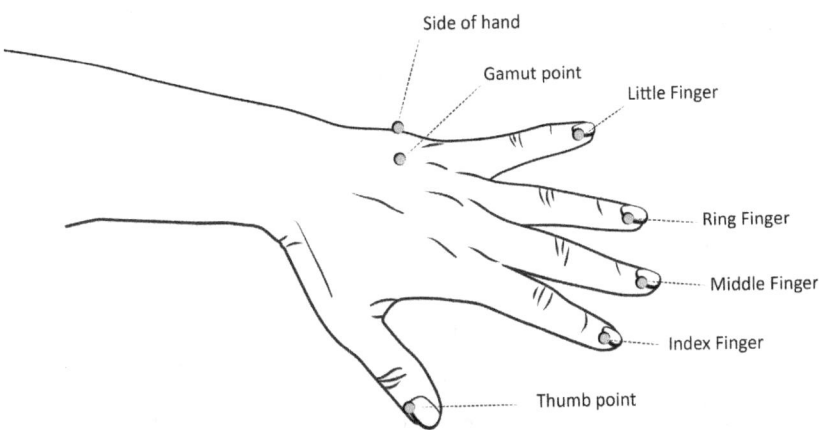

EMOTION LIST

Confusion	Sad	Strong
Uncertain	Depressed	Sure
Upset	Desperate	Certain
Doubtful	Dejected	Unique
Uncertain	Heavy	Dynamic
Indecisive	Crushed	Tenacious
Perplexed	Disgusted	Hardy
Embarrassed	Upset	Secure
Hesitant	Hateful	Empowered
Shy	Sorrowful	Ambitious
Lost	Mournful	Powerful
Unsure	Weepy	Confident
Pessimistic	Frustrated	Bold
Tense		Determined
	Anger	
Happy	Annoyed	
Amused	Agitated	Energised
Delighted	Fed Up	Determined
Glad	Irritated	Inspired
Pleased	Mad	Creative
Charmed	Critical	Healthy
Grateful	Resentful	Renewed
Optimistic	Disgusted	Vibrant
Content	Outraged	Strengthened
Joyful	Raging	Motivated
Enthusiastic	Furious	Focused
Loving	Livid	Invigorated
Marvellous	Bitter	Refreshed

AFFIRMATIONS AND CHOICES

List some affirmation and choices that you want to include in your tapping to support your grounding and feeling of safety.

_____

_____

_____

_____

_____

_____

_____

_____

_____

_____

_____

_____

_____

_____

AFFIRMATIONS AND CHOICES

AFFIRMATIONS AND CHOICES

Chapter Two

The Basic Recipe

IDENTIFYING YOUR SUDS

SUBJECT UNITS OF DISTRESS

1 On a scale from 0 to 10 — with 0 being no intensity and 10 being the most extreme — rate the intensity of the emotion you're focusing on right now.

2 Now you know your issue and emotion you would like to tap on, I invite you to bring your attention to your issue, how it feels within your body and give it a number on a scale from 0 – 10. 10 being the most intense and 0 being you don't feel distress at all.

3 Don't think too in depth with what the number may be. There is no right or wrong answer. Use your intuition. The first number that comes to you when you bring awareness to your issue and how it feels within your body.

10 STEPS OF THE BASIC RECIPE

1 Decide on the event/ issue/ challenge you would like to tap on and the emotion behind it. You may write down how you feel within your body regarding this event/ issue/ challenge.

2 Identify your SUDS. You rate it out of 10.

3 Create a set up statement and whilst tapping on the side of the hand say the set up statement three (3) times.

4 Tap your rounds using reminder phrases

As you tap on each point, you state something from your full sequence, from the list of things that came up when attuning to how you feel within your body, where in the body it is felt, anything else that may come up during the tapping and/ or any shifts in perception.

5 After 1-3 rounds, or where you feel is needed, check in with yourself and your rating out of 10. (SUDS)

6 Tap more rounds depending on your rating. Repeating stages 4 and 5 as many times as you need.

Once we have tapped for a few rounds, hopefully you're finding your SUDS are moving and you might have a bit of a perspective shift happening.

7 Tapping on affirmations and choices

8 Check in with your rating, your SUDS. If needed repeat more rounds.

9 Seal your tapping practice with a deep inhale and exhale with a sigh.

10 Allow any insights and/or reflections to arise. Inviting you to write anything down if needed.

DATE:

BASIC RECIPE

EXPERIENCE/ ISSUE/ EVENT/ CHAKRA/ CHALLENGE I WANT TO WORK ON

EMOTIONS ATTACHED?
WHAT IS BENEATH THE EMOTION?

SET UP STATEMENT

SUDS

WHERE IS IT LOCATED IN THE BODY?
SCAN THE BODY. ANY SENSATIONS? TENSIONS? ETC.
COLOUR/ SIZE/ SHAPE/ TEMPERATURE/ TEXTURE/ WEIGHT/ SMELL/ TASTE?

AFFIRMATIONS AND CHOICES

INSIGHTS AND REFLECTIONS

OTHER EXPERIENCE/ ISSUE/ EVENT/ CHAKRA/ CHALLENGE THAT CAME THROUGH IN THE TAPPING ROUND?

DATE:

BASIC RECIPE

EXPERIENCE/ ISSUE/ EVENT/ CHAKRA/ CHALLENGE I WANT TO WORK ON

EMOTIONS ATTACHED?
WHAT IS BENEATH THE EMOTION?

SET UP STATEMENT

SUDS

WHERE IS IT LOCATED IN THE BODY?
SCAN THE BODY. ANY SENSATIONS? TENSIONS? ETC.
COLOUR/ SIZE/ SHAPE/ TEMPERATURE/ TEXTURE/ WEIGHT/ SMELL/ TASTE?

AFFIRMATIONS AND CHOICES

INSIGHTS AND REFLECTIONS

OTHER EXPERIENCE/ ISSUE/ EVENT/ CHAKRA/ CHALLENGE THAT CAME THROUGH IN THE TAPPING ROUND?

DATE:

BASIC RECIPE

EXPERIENCE/ ISSUE/ EVENT/ CHAKRA/ CHALLENGE I WANT TO WORK ON

EMOTIONS ATTACHED?
WHAT IS BENEATH THE EMOTION?

SET UP STATEMENT

SUDS

WHERE IS IT LOCATED IN THE BODY?
SCAN THE BODY. ANY SENSATIONS? TENSIONS? ETC.
COLOUR/ SIZE/ SHAPE/ TEMPERATURE/ TEXTURE/ WEIGHT/ SMELL/ TASTE?

AFFIRMATIONS AND CHOICES

INSIGHTS AND REFLECTIONS

OTHER EXPERIENCE/ ISSUE/ EVENT/ CHAKRA/ CHALLENGE THAT CAME THROUGH IN THE TAPPING ROUND?

DATE:

BASIC RECIPE

EXPERIENCE/ ISSUE/ EVENT/ CHAKRA/ CHALLENGE I WANT TO WORK ON

EMOTIONS ATTACHED?
WHAT IS BENEATH THE EMOTION?

SET UP STATEMENT

SUDS

WHERE IS IT LOCATED IN THE BODY?
SCAN THE BODY. ANY SENSATIONS? TENSIONS? ETC.
COLOUR/ SIZE/ SHAPE/ TEMPERATURE/ TEXTURE/ WEIGHT/ SMELL/ TASTE?

AFFIRMATIONS AND CHOICES

INSIGHTS AND REFLECTIONS

OTHER EXPERIENCE/ ISSUE/ EVENT/ CHAKRA/ CHALLENGE THAT CAME THROUGH IN THE TAPPING ROUND?

DATE:

BASIC RECIPE

EXPERIENCE/ ISSUE/ EVENT/ CHAKRA/ CHALLENGE I WANT TO WORK ON

EMOTIONS ATTACHED?
WHAT IS BENEATH THE EMOTION?

SET UP STATEMENT

SUDS

WHERE IS IT LOCATED IN THE BODY?
SCAN THE BODY. ANY SENSATIONS? TENSIONS? ETC.
COLOUR/ SIZE/ SHAPE/ TEMPERATURE/ TEXTURE/ WEIGHT/ SMELL/ TASTE?

AFFIRMATIONS AND CHOICES

INSIGHTS AND REFLECTIONS

OTHER EXPERIENCE/ ISSUE/ EVENT/ CHAKRA/ CHALLENGE THAT CAME THROUGH IN THE TAPPING ROUND?

DATE:

BASIC RECIPE

EXPERIENCE/ ISSUE/ EVENT/ CHAKRA/ CHALLENGE I WANT TO WORK ON

EMOTIONS ATTACHED?
WHAT IS BENEATH THE EMOTION?

SET UP STATEMENT

SUDS

WHERE IS IT LOCATED IN THE BODY?
SCAN THE BODY. ANY SENSATIONS? TENSIONS? ETC.
COLOUR/ SIZE/ SHAPE/ TEMPERATURE/ TEXTURE/ WEIGHT/ SMELL/ TASTE?

AFFIRMATIONS AND CHOICES

INSIGHTS AND REFLECTIONS

OTHER EXPERIENCE/ ISSUE/ EVENT/ CHAKRA/ CHALLENGE THAT CAME THROUGH IN THE TAPPING ROUND?

DATE:

BASIC RECIPE

EXPERIENCE/ ISSUE/ EVENT/ CHAKRA/ CHALLENGE I WANT TO WORK ON

EMOTIONS ATTACHED?
WHAT IS BENEATH THE EMOTION?

SET UP STATEMENT

SUDS

WHERE IS IT LOCATED IN THE BODY?
SCAN THE BODY. ANY SENSATIONS? TENSIONS? ETC.
COLOUR/ SIZE/ SHAPE/ TEMPERATURE/ TEXTURE/ WEIGHT/ SMELL/ TASTE?

AFFIRMATIONS AND CHOICES

INSIGHTS AND REFLECTIONS

OTHER EXPERIENCE/ ISSUE/ EVENT/ CHAKRA/ CHALLENGE THAT CAME THROUGH IN THE TAPPING ROUND?

Chapter Three

Tapping Through the Layers

LIMITING BELIEFS

List the limiting beliefs that arise for you. Some you may know straight away and others may become known to you as they appear through when tapping.

Being aware of your limiting beliefs will enable you to meet and release them, as you go through the layers of your healing journey.

_____
_____
_____
_____
_____
_____
_____
_____
_____
_____
_____
_____
_____
_____
_____
_____
_____

LIMITING BELIEFS

LIMITING BELIEFS

TAPPING TREE

Title - Naming your Tapping Tree

_____

Leaves - Symptoms/ Other side effects

_____

_____

Branches - Emotions you feel about the issue

_____

_____

Trunk - Events we use as proof

_____

_____

Roots - Limiting beliefs

_____

_____

NOTES

DATE:

BASIC RECIPE

EXPERIENCE/ ISSUE/ EVENT/ CHAKRA/ CHALLENGE I WANT TO WORK ON

EMOTIONS ATTACHED?
WHAT IS BENEATH THE EMOTION?

SET UP STATEMENT

SUDS

WHERE IS IT LOCATED IN THE BODY?
SCAN THE BODY. ANY SENSATIONS? TENSIONS? ETC.
COLOUR/ SIZE/ SHAPE/ TEMPERATURE/ TEXTURE/ WEIGHT/ SMELL/ TASTE?

AFFIRMATIONS AND CHOICES

INSIGHTS AND REFLECTIONS

OTHER EXPERIENCE/ ISSUE/ EVENT/ CHAKRA/ CHALLENGE THAT CAME THROUGH IN THE TAPPING ROUND?

TAPPING TREE

Title - Naming your Tapping Tree

_____

Leaves - Symptoms/ Other side effects

_____

_____

Branches - Emotions you feel about the issue

_____

_____

Trunk - Events we use as proof

_____

_____

Roots - Limiting beliefs

_____

_____

NOTES

DATE:

BASIC RECIPE

EXPERIENCE/ ISSUE/ EVENT/ CHAKRA/ CHALLENGE I WANT TO WORK ON

EMOTIONS ATTACHED?
WHAT IS BENEATH THE EMOTION?

SET UP STATEMENT

SUDS

WHERE IS IT LOCATED IN THE BODY?
SCAN THE BODY. ANY SENSATIONS? TENSIONS? ETC.
COLOUR/ SIZE/ SHAPE/ TEMPERATURE/ TEXTURE/ WEIGHT/ SMELL/ TASTE?

AFFIRMATIONS AND CHOICES

INSIGHTS AND REFLECTIONS

OTHER EXPERIENCE/ ISSUE/ EVENT/ CHAKRA/ CHALLENGE THAT CAME THROUGH IN THE TAPPING ROUND?

TAPPING TREE

Title - Naming your Tapping Tree

_____

Leaves - Symptoms/ Other side effects

_____

_____

Branches - Emotions you feel about the issue

_____

_____

Trunk - Events we use as proof

_____

_____

Roots - Limiting beliefs

_____

_____

NOTES

DATE:

BASIC RECIPE

EXPERIENCE/ ISSUE/ EVENT/ CHAKRA/ CHALLENGE I WANT TO WORK ON

EMOTIONS ATTACHED?
WHAT IS BENEATH THE EMOTION?

SET UP STATEMENT

SUDS

WHERE IS IT LOCATED IN THE BODY?
SCAN THE BODY. ANY SENSATIONS? TENSIONS? ETC.
COLOUR/ SIZE/ SHAPE/ TEMPERATURE/ TEXTURE/ WEIGHT/ SMELL/ TASTE?

AFFIRMATIONS AND CHOICES

INSIGHTS AND REFLECTIONS

OTHER EXPERIENCE/ ISSUE/ EVENT/ CHAKRA/ CHALLENGE THAT CAME THROUGH IN THE TAPPING ROUND?

TAPPING TREE

Title - Naming your Tapping Tree

_____

Leaves - Symptoms/ Other side effects

_____

_____

Branches - Emotions you feel about the issue

_____

_____

Trunk - Events we use as proof

_____

_____

Roots - Limiting beliefs

_____

_____

NOTES

DATE:

BASIC RECIPE

EXPERIENCE/ ISSUE/ EVENT/ CHAKRA/ CHALLENGE I WANT TO WORK ON

EMOTIONS ATTACHED?
WHAT IS BENEATH THE EMOTION?

SET UP STATEMENT

SUDS

WHERE IS IT LOCATED IN THE BODY?
SCAN THE BODY. ANY SENSATIONS? TENSIONS? ETC.
COLOUR/ SIZE/ SHAPE/ TEMPERATURE/ TEXTURE/ WEIGHT/ SMELL/ TASTE?

AFFIRMATIONS AND CHOICES

INSIGHTS AND REFLECTIONS

OTHER EXPERIENCE/ ISSUE/ EVENT/ CHAKRA/ CHALLENGE THAT CAME THROUGH IN THE TAPPING ROUND?

TAPPING TREE

Title - Naming your Tapping Tree

_____

Leaves - Symptoms/ Other side effects

_____

_____

Branches - Emotions you feel about the issue

_____

_____

Trunk - Events we use as proof

_____

_____

Roots - Limiting beliefs

_____

_____

NOTES

DATE:

BASIC RECIPE

EXPERIENCE/ ISSUE/ EVENT/ CHAKRA/ CHALLENGE I WANT TO WORK ON

EMOTIONS ATTACHED?
WHAT IS BENEATH THE EMOTION?

SET UP STATEMENT

SUDS

WHERE IS IT LOCATED IN THE BODY?
SCAN THE BODY. ANY SENSATIONS? TENSIONS? ETC.
COLOUR/ SIZE/ SHAPE/ TEMPERATURE/ TEXTURE/ WEIGHT/ SMELL/ TASTE?

AFFIRMATIONS AND CHOICES

INSIGHTS AND REFLECTIONS

OTHER EXPERIENCE/ ISSUE/ EVENT/ CHAKRA/ CHALLENGE THAT CAME THROUGH IN THE TAPPING ROUND?

TAPPING TREE

Title - Naming your Tapping Tree

_____

Leaves - Symptoms/ Other side effects

_____

_____

Branches - Emotions you feel about the issue

_____

_____

Trunk - Events we use as proof

_____

_____

Roots - Limiting beliefs

_____

_____

NOTES

DATE:

BASIC RECIPE

EXPERIENCE/ ISSUE/ EVENT/ CHAKRA/ CHALLENGE I WANT TO WORK ON

EMOTIONS ATTACHED?
WHAT IS BENEATH THE EMOTION?

SET UP STATEMENT

SUDS

WHERE IS IT LOCATED IN THE BODY?
SCAN THE BODY. ANY SENSATIONS? TENSIONS? ETC.
COLOUR/ SIZE/ SHAPE/ TEMPERATURE/ TEXTURE/ WEIGHT/ SMELL/ TASTE?

AFFIRMATIONS AND CHOICES

INSIGHTS AND REFLECTIONS

OTHER EXPERIENCE/ ISSUE/ EVENT/ CHAKRA/ CHALLENGE THAT CAME THROUGH IN THE TAPPING ROUND?

TAPPING TREE

Title - Naming your Tapping Tree

_____

Leaves - Symptoms/ Other side effects

_____

_____

Branches - Emotions you feel about the issue

_____

_____

Trunk - Events we use as proof

_____

_____

Roots - Limiting beliefs

_____

_____

NOTES

DATE:

BASIC RECIPE

EXPERIENCE/ ISSUE/ EVENT/ CHAKRA/
CHALLENGE I WANT TO WORK ON

EMOTIONS ATTACHED?
WHAT IS BENEATH THE EMOTION?

SET UP STATEMENT

SUDS

WHERE IS IT LOCATED IN THE BODY?
SCAN THE BODY. ANY SENSATIONS? TENSIONS? ETC.
COLOUR/ SIZE/ SHAPE/ TEMPERATURE/ TEXTURE/ WEIGHT/ SMELL/ TASTE?

AFFIRMATIONS AND CHOICES

INSIGHTS AND REFLECTIONS

OTHER EXPERIENCE/ ISSUE/ EVENT/ CHAKRA/ CHALLENGE THAT CAME THROUGH IN THE TAPPING ROUND?

Chapter Four

Personal Peace Procedure

PERSONAL PEACE PROCEDURE

MOVIE TITLE	SUDS	TRAFFIC LIGHT RATING

PERSONAL PEACE PROCEDURE

MOVIE TITLE	SUDS	TRAFFIC LIGHT RATING

PERSONAL PEACE PROCEDURE

MOVIE TITLE	SUDS	TRAFFIC LIGHT RATING

DATE:

BASIC RECIPE

EXPERIENCE/ ISSUE/ EVENT/ CHAKRA/ CHALLENGE I WANT TO WORK ON

EMOTIONS ATTACHED?
WHAT IS BENEATH THE EMOTION?

SET UP STATEMENT

SUDS

WHERE IS IT LOCATED IN THE BODY?
SCAN THE BODY. ANY SENSATIONS? TENSIONS? ETC.
COLOUR/ SIZE/ SHAPE/ TEMPERATURE/ TEXTURE/ WEIGHT/ SMELL/ TASTE?

AFFIRMATIONS AND CHOICES

INSIGHTS AND REFLECTIONS

OTHER EXPERIENCE/ ISSUE/ EVENT/ CHAKRA/ CHALLENGE THAT CAME THROUGH IN THE TAPPING ROUND?

DATE:

BASIC RECIPE

EXPERIENCE/ ISSUE/ EVENT/ CHAKRA/ CHALLENGE I WANT TO WORK ON

EMOTIONS ATTACHED?
WHAT IS BENEATH THE EMOTION?

SET UP STATEMENT

SUDS

WHERE IS IT LOCATED IN THE BODY?
SCAN THE BODY. ANY SENSATIONS? TENSIONS? ETC.
COLOUR/ SIZE/ SHAPE/ TEMPERATURE/ TEXTURE/ WEIGHT/ SMELL/ TASTE?

AFFIRMATIONS AND CHOICES

INSIGHTS AND REFLECTIONS

OTHER EXPERIENCE/ ISSUE/ EVENT/ CHAKRA/ CHALLENGE THAT CAME THROUGH IN THE TAPPING ROUND?

DATE:

BASIC RECIPE

EXPERIENCE/ ISSUE/ EVENT/ CHAKRA/ CHALLENGE I WANT TO WORK ON

EMOTIONS ATTACHED?
WHAT IS BENEATH THE EMOTION?

SET UP STATEMENT

SUDS

WHERE IS IT LOCATED IN THE BODY?
SCAN THE BODY. ANY SENSATIONS? TENSIONS? ETC.
COLOUR/ SIZE/ SHAPE/ TEMPERATURE/ TEXTURE/ WEIGHT/ SMELL/ TASTE?

AFFIRMATIONS AND CHOICES

INSIGHTS AND REFLECTIONS

OTHER EXPERIENCE/ ISSUE/ EVENT/ CHAKRA/ CHALLENGE THAT CAME THROUGH IN THE TAPPING ROUND?

DATE:

BASIC RECIPE

EXPERIENCE/ ISSUE/ EVENT/ CHAKRA/
CHALLENGE I WANT TO WORK ON

EMOTIONS ATTACHED?
WHAT IS BENEATH THE EMOTION?

SET UP STATEMENT

SUDS

WHERE IS IT LOCATED IN THE BODY?
SCAN THE BODY. ANY SENSATIONS? TENSIONS? ETC.
COLOUR/ SIZE/ SHAPE/ TEMPERATURE/ TEXTURE/ WEIGHT/ SMELL/ TASTE?

AFFIRMATIONS AND CHOICES

INSIGHTS AND REFLECTIONS

OTHER EXPERIENCE/ ISSUE/ EVENT/ CHAKRA/ CHALLENGE THAT CAME THROUGH IN THE TAPPING ROUND?

DATE:

BASIC RECIPE

EXPERIENCE/ ISSUE/ EVENT/ CHAKRA/ CHALLENGE I WANT TO WORK ON

EMOTIONS ATTACHED?
WHAT IS BENEATH THE EMOTION?

SET UP STATEMENT

SUDS

WHERE IS IT LOCATED IN THE BODY?
SCAN THE BODY. ANY SENSATIONS? TENSIONS? ETC.
COLOUR/ SIZE/ SHAPE/ TEMPERATURE/ TEXTURE/ WEIGHT/ SMELL/ TASTE?

AFFIRMATIONS AND CHOICES

INSIGHTS AND REFLECTIONS

OTHER EXPERIENCE/ ISSUE/ EVENT/ CHAKRA/ CHALLENGE THAT CAME THROUGH IN THE TAPPING ROUND?

DATE:

BASIC RECIPE

EXPERIENCE/ ISSUE/ EVENT/ CHAKRA/ CHALLENGE I WANT TO WORK ON

EMOTIONS ATTACHED?
WHAT IS BENEATH THE EMOTION?

SET UP STATEMENT

SUDS

WHERE IS IT LOCATED IN THE BODY?
SCAN THE BODY. ANY SENSATIONS? TENSIONS? ETC.
COLOUR/ SIZE/ SHAPE/ TEMPERATURE/ TEXTURE/ WEIGHT/ SMELL/ TASTE?

AFFIRMATIONS AND CHOICES

INSIGHTS AND REFLECTIONS

OTHER EXPERIENCE/ ISSUE/ EVENT/ CHAKRA/ CHALLENGE THAT CAME THROUGH IN THE TAPPING ROUND?

DATE:

BASIC RECIPE

EXPERIENCE/ ISSUE/ EVENT/ CHAKRA/ CHALLENGE I WANT TO WORK ON

EMOTIONS ATTACHED?
WHAT IS BENEATH THE EMOTION?

SET UP STATEMENT

SUDS

WHERE IS IT LOCATED IN THE BODY?
SCAN THE BODY. ANY SENSATIONS? TENSIONS? ETC.
COLOUR/ SIZE/ SHAPE/ TEMPERATURE/ TEXTURE/ WEIGHT/ SMELL/ TASTE?

AFFIRMATIONS AND CHOICES

INSIGHTS AND REFLECTIONS

OTHER EXPERIENCE/ ISSUE/ EVENT/ CHAKRA/ CHALLENGE THAT CAME THROUGH IN THE TAPPING ROUND?

Chapter Five

Chakra Tapping

LOCATION OF YOUR CHAKRAS

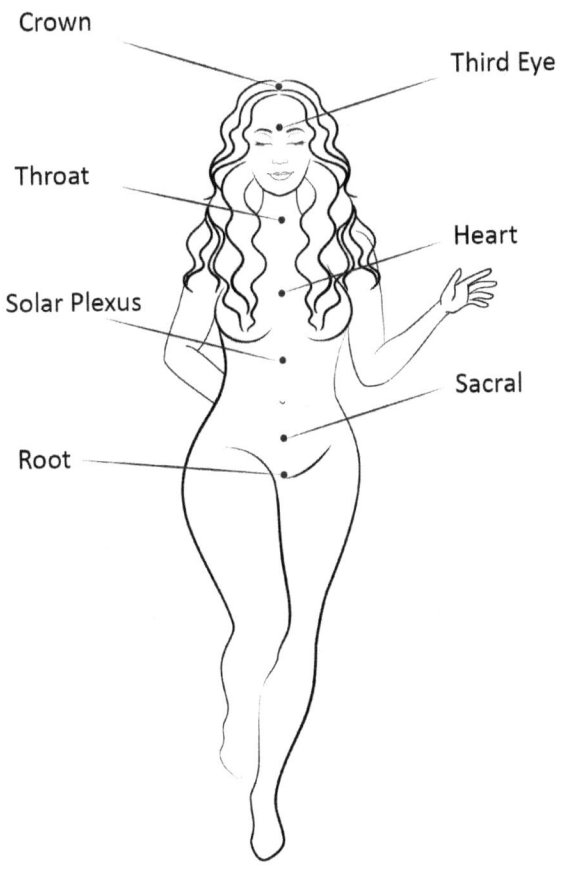

AFFIRMATIONS AND CHOICES

List some affirmation and choices that you want to include in your tapping to support your chakras.

AFFIRMATIONS AND CHOICES

10 STEPS OF THE CHAKRA BASIC RECIPE

1 Decide on the chakra you would like to tap on and the emotion behind it. You may write down how you feel within your body regarding this chakra.

2 Identify your SUDS. You rate it out of 10.

3 Create a set up statement and whilst tapping on the side of the hand say the set up statement three (3) times.

4 tap on your rounds using reminder phrases

As you tap on each point, you state something from your full sequence, from the list of things that came up when attuning to how you feel about that part of the chakra, where in the body it is felt, anything else that may come up during the tapping and/ or any shifts in perception.

5 After 1-3 rounds, or where you feel is needed, rate your intensity out of 10 - check SUDS

6 Tapping on affirmations and choices

Once we have tapped for a few rounds, hopefully you're finding your SUDS are moving and you might have a bit of a perspective shift happening.

7 Rate the intensity again – check SUDS again

8 Attune to your chosen chakra for one (1) minute

9 Seal your tapping process with a deep inhale and exhale with a sigh

10 Allow any insights and/or reflections to arise. Inviting you to write anything down if needed.

DATE:

BASIC RECIPE

EXPERIENCE/ ISSUE/ EVENT/ CHAKRA/ CHALLENGE I WANT TO WORK ON

EMOTIONS ATTACHED?
WHAT IS BENEATH THE EMOTION?

SET UP STATEMENT

SUDS

WHERE IS IT LOCATED IN THE BODY?
SCAN THE BODY. ANY SENSATIONS? TENSIONS? ETC.
COLOUR/ SIZE/ SHAPE/ TEMPERATURE/ TEXTURE/ WEIGHT/ SMELL/ TASTE?

AFFIRMATIONS AND CHOICES

INSIGHTS AND REFLECTIONS

OTHER EXPERIENCE/ ISSUE/ EVENT/ CHAKRA/ CHALLENGE THAT CAME THROUGH IN THE TAPPING ROUND?

DATE:

BASIC RECIPE

EXPERIENCE/ ISSUE/ EVENT/ CHAKRA/ CHALLENGE I WANT TO WORK ON

EMOTIONS ATTACHED?
WHAT IS BENEATH THE EMOTION?

SET UP STATEMENT

SUDS

WHERE IS IT LOCATED IN THE BODY?
SCAN THE BODY. ANY SENSATIONS? TENSIONS? ETC.
COLOUR/ SIZE/ SHAPE/ TEMPERATURE/ TEXTURE/ WEIGHT/ SMELL/ TASTE?

AFFIRMATIONS AND CHOICES

INSIGHTS AND REFLECTIONS

OTHER EXPERIENCE/ ISSUE/ EVENT/ CHAKRA/ CHALLENGE THAT CAME THROUGH IN THE TAPPING ROUND?

DATE:

BASIC RECIPE

EXPERIENCE/ ISSUE/ EVENT/ CHAKRA/ CHALLENGE I WANT TO WORK ON

EMOTIONS ATTACHED?
WHAT IS BENEATH THE EMOTION?

SET UP STATEMENT

SUDS

WHERE IS IT LOCATED IN THE BODY?
SCAN THE BODY. ANY SENSATIONS? TENSIONS? ETC.
COLOUR/ SIZE/ SHAPE/ TEMPERATURE/ TEXTURE/ WEIGHT/ SMELL/ TASTE?

AFFIRMATIONS AND CHOICES

INSIGHTS AND REFLECTIONS

OTHER EXPERIENCE/ ISSUE/ EVENT/ CHAKRA/ CHALLENGE THAT CAME THROUGH IN THE TAPPING ROUND?

DATE:

BASIC RECIPE

EXPERIENCE/ ISSUE/ EVENT/ CHAKRA/ CHALLENGE I WANT TO WORK ON

EMOTIONS ATTACHED?
WHAT IS BENEATH THE EMOTION?

SET UP STATEMENT

SUDS

WHERE IS IT LOCATED IN THE BODY?
SCAN THE BODY. ANY SENSATIONS? TENSIONS? ETC.
COLOUR/ SIZE/ SHAPE/ TEMPERATURE/ TEXTURE/ WEIGHT/ SMELL/ TASTE?

AFFIRMATIONS AND CHOICES

INSIGHTS AND REFLECTIONS

OTHER EXPERIENCE/ ISSUE/ EVENT/ CHAKRA/ CHALLENGE THAT CAME THROUGH IN THE TAPPING ROUND?

DATE:

BASIC RECIPE

EXPERIENCE/ ISSUE/ EVENT/ CHAKRA/ CHALLENGE I WANT TO WORK ON

EMOTIONS ATTACHED?
WHAT IS BENEATH THE EMOTION?

SET UP STATEMENT

SUDS

WHERE IS IT LOCATED IN THE BODY?
SCAN THE BODY. ANY SENSATIONS? TENSIONS? ETC.
COLOUR/ SIZE/ SHAPE/ TEMPERATURE/ TEXTURE/ WEIGHT/ SMELL/ TASTE?

AFFIRMATIONS AND CHOICES

INSIGHTS AND REFLECTIONS

OTHER EXPERIENCE/ ISSUE/ EVENT/ CHAKRA/ CHALLENGE THAT CAME THROUGH IN THE TAPPING ROUND?

DATE:

BASIC RECIPE

EXPERIENCE/ ISSUE/ EVENT/ CHAKRA/ CHALLENGE I WANT TO WORK ON

EMOTIONS ATTACHED?
WHAT IS BENEATH THE EMOTION?

SET UP STATEMENT

SUDS

WHERE IS IT LOCATED IN THE BODY?
SCAN THE BODY. ANY SENSATIONS? TENSIONS? ETC.
COLOUR/ SIZE/ SHAPE/ TEMPERATURE/ TEXTURE/ WEIGHT/ SMELL/ TASTE?

AFFIRMATIONS AND CHOICES

INSIGHTS AND REFLECTIONS

OTHER EXPERIENCE/ ISSUE/ EVENT/ CHAKRA/ CHALLENGE THAT CAME THROUGH IN THE TAPPING ROUND?

DATE:

BASIC RECIPE

EXPERIENCE/ ISSUE/ EVENT/ CHAKRA/ CHALLENGE I WANT TO WORK ON

EMOTIONS ATTACHED?
WHAT IS BENEATH THE EMOTION?

SET UP STATEMENT

SUDS

WHERE IS IT LOCATED IN THE BODY?
SCAN THE BODY. ANY SENSATIONS? TENSIONS? ETC.
COLOUR/ SIZE/ SHAPE/ TEMPERATURE/ TEXTURE/ WEIGHT/ SMELL/ TASTE?

AFFIRMATIONS AND CHOICES

INSIGHTS AND REFLECTIONS

OTHER EXPERIENCE/ ISSUE/ EVENT/ CHAKRA/ CHALLENGE THAT CAME THROUGH IN THE TAPPING ROUND?

Chapter Six

Other Tapping Practices

WITNESS TAPPING

Write down your notes and reflections on how it felt to try Witness Tapping

IMAGINAL TAPPING

Write down your notes and reflections on how it felt to try Imaginal Tapping

SUBTLE TAPPING

Write down your notes and reflections on how it felt to try Subtle Tapping

_____
_____
_____
_____
_____
_____
_____
_____
_____
_____
_____
_____
_____
_____
_____
_____
_____

CONTINUAL TAPPING

Write down your notes and reflections on how it felt to try Continual Tapping.

BECOMING AWARE CHECKLIST

Give yourself permission to bring awareness to how you may rest and/ or how you are in a stressed state.

Where are your hands resting?

When you find your hands resting near/ on a tapping point, allow yourself to do some tapping (in whichever way feels comfortable for you) on that point for one (1) minute.

See if you can tick off everyone tapping point by bringing awareness to yourself on where your hands are resting throughout your day.

MAIN TAPPING POINTS

- [ ] EYEBROW POINT
- [ ] SIDE OF EYE POINT
- [ ] UNDER EYE POINT
- [ ] UNDER NOSE POINT
- [ ] CHIN POINT
- [ ] COLLAR BONE POINT
- [ ] UNDER ARM POINT
- [ ] STOP OF HEAD POINT

ADDITIONAL TAPPING POINTS

- [ ] GAMUT POINT
- [ ] HEART CENTRE POINT
- [ ] WRIST POINT

FINGER TAPPING POINTS

- [ ] THUMB POINT
- [ ] GOING THROUGH ALL THE FINGER POINT ON BOTH HANDS
- [ ] GOING THROUGH ALL THE FINGER POINTS ON ONE HAND
- [ ] GOING THROUGH ALL THE FINGER POINTS ON ONE HAND USING ONE HAND

Chapter Seven

Inviting Tapping into Your Life

WEEKLY REVIEW

List your scheduling you have for each day to help you identify ways you can invite tapping into your life.
Eg: Work days, kids swimming lessons etc

SUNDAY

MONDAY

TUESDAY

WEDNESDAY

THURSDAY

FRIDAY

SATURDAY

30 DAY PRACTICE

Bring awareness to your life and your daily routines. Where can you incorporate tapping into your life? Write down 20-50 different ways you can incorporate tapping into your life.

_____
_____
_____
_____
_____
_____
_____
_____
_____
_____
_____
_____
_____
_____
_____
_____
_____
_____
_____
_____

30 DAY PRACTICE

30 DAY PRACTICE

INVITING TAPPING PRACTICES INTO YOUR LIFE
30-DAY CHECKLIST

01	02	03	04	05
06	07	08	09	10
11	12	13	14	15
16	17	18	19	20
21	22	23	24	25
26	27	28	29	30

DATE:

DAY 1

WAYS I INCORPORATED TAPPING INTO MY LIFE TODAY

- ☐ BASIC RECIPE
- ☐ PERSONAL PEACE PROCEDURE
- ☐ WITNESS TAPPING
- ☐ CHAKRA TAPPING
- ☐ SUBTLE TAPPING
- ☐ IMAGINAL TAPPING
- ☐ CONTINUAL TAPPING
- ☐ BORROWED BENEFITS

BEGINNING OF MY DAY
WHAT EMOTION DO I FEEL AND WHERE DO I FEEL IT IN MY BODY?

END OF MY DAY
WHAT EMOTION DO I FEEL AND WHERE DO I FEEL IT IN MY BODY?

INSIGHTS AND REFLECTIONS

3 THINGS I FEEL GRATEFUL TODAY ARE

_____

_____

_____

ONE MINUTE PRACTICE

Give yourself permission to tap on any point/s that feel comfortable for you whilst saying, 'I choose to show up for myself.'

NOTES

DATE:

BASIC RECIPE

EXPERIENCE/ ISSUE/ EVENT/ CHAKRA/
CHALLENGE I WANT TO WORK ON

EMOTIONS ATTACHED?
WHAT IS BENEATH THE EMOTION?

SET UP STATEMENT

SUDS

WHERE IS IT LOCATED IN THE BODY?
SCAN THE BODY. ANY SENSATIONS? TENSIONS? ETC.
COLOUR/ SIZE/ SHAPE/ TEMPERATURE/ TEXTURE/ WEIGHT/ SMELL/ TASTE?

AFFIRMATIONS AND CHOICES

INSIGHTS AND REFLECTIONS

OTHER EXPERIENCE/ ISSUE/ EVENT/ CHAKRA/ CHALLENGE THAT CAME THROUGH IN THE TAPPING ROUND?

DATE:

DAY 2

WAYS I INCORPORATED TAPPING INTO MY LIFE TODAY

- ☐ BASIC RECIPE
- ☐ PERSONAL PEACE PROCEDURE
- ☐ WITNESS TAPPING
- ☐ CHAKRA TAPPING

- ☐ SUBTLE TAPPING
- ☐ IMAGINAL TAPPING
- ☐ CONTINUAL TAPPING
- ☐ BORROWED BENEFITS

BEGINNING OF MY DAY
WHAT EMOTION DO I FEEL AND WHERE DO I FEEL IT IN MY BODY?

END OF MY DAY
WHAT EMOTION DO I FEEL AND WHERE DO I FEEL IT IN MY BODY?

INSIGHTS AND REFLECTIONS

3 THINGS I FEEL GRATEFUL TODAY ARE

_____
_____
_____

ONE MINUTE PRACTICE

Give yourself permission to tap on any point/s that feel comfortable for you whilst saying, 'I choose to allow myself grace.'

NOTES

DATE:

BASIC RECIPE

EXPERIENCE/ ISSUE/ EVENT/ CHAKRA/
CHALLENGE I WANT TO WORK ON

EMOTIONS ATTACHED?
WHAT IS BENEATH THE EMOTION?

SET UP STATEMENT

SUDS

WHERE IS IT LOCATED IN THE BODY?
SCAN THE BODY. ANY SENSATIONS? TENSIONS? ETC.
COLOUR/ SIZE/ SHAPE/ TEMPERATURE/ TEXTURE/ WEIGHT/ SMELL/ TASTE?

AFFIRMATIONS AND CHOICES

INSIGHTS AND REFLECTIONS

OTHER EXPERIENCE/ ISSUE/ EVENT/ CHAKRA/ CHALLENGE THAT CAME THROUGH IN THE TAPPING ROUND?

DATE:

DAY 3

WAYS I INCORPORATED TAPPING INTO MY LIFE TODAY

- ☐ BASIC RECIPE
- ☐ PERSONAL PEACE PROCEDURE
- ☐ WITNESS TAPPING
- ☐ CHAKRA TAPPING
- ☐ SUBTLE TAPPING
- ☐ IMAGINAL TAPPING
- ☐ CONTINUAL TAPPING
- ☐ BORROWED BENEFITS

BEGINNING OF MY DAY
WHAT EMOTION DO I FEEL AND WHERE DO I FEEL IT IN MY BODY?

END OF MY DAY
WHAT EMOTION DO I FEEL AND WHERE DO I FEEL IT IN MY BODY?

INSIGHTS AND REFLECTIONS

3 THINGS I FEEL GRATEFUL TODAY ARE

_____
_____
_____

ONE MINUTE PRACTICE

Give yourself permission to tap on any point/s that feel comfortable for you whilst saying, 'I choose to become an active participant in my own healing.'

NOTES

DATE:

BASIC RECIPE

EXPERIENCE/ ISSUE/ EVENT/ CHAKRA/ CHALLENGE I WANT TO WORK ON

EMOTIONS ATTACHED?
WHAT IS BENEATH THE EMOTION?

SET UP STATEMENT

SUDS

WHERE IS IT LOCATED IN THE BODY?
SCAN THE BODY. ANY SENSATIONS? TENSIONS? ETC.
COLOUR/ SIZE/ SHAPE/ TEMPERATURE/ TEXTURE/ WEIGHT/ SMELL/ TASTE?

AFFIRMATIONS AND CHOICES

INSIGHTS AND REFLECTIONS

OTHER EXPERIENCE/ ISSUE/ EVENT/ CHAKRA/ CHALLENGE THAT CAME THROUGH IN THE TAPPING ROUND?

DATE:

DAY 4

WAYS I INCORPORATED TAPPING INTO MY LIFE TODAY

- [ ] BASIC RECIPE
- [ ] PERSONAL PEACE PROCEDURE
- [ ] WITNESS TAPPING
- [ ] CHAKRA TAPPING
- [ ] SUBTLE TAPPING
- [ ] IMAGINAL TAPPING
- [ ] CONTINUAL TAPPING
- [ ] BORROWED BENEFITS

BEGINNING OF MY DAY
WHAT EMOTION DO I FEEL AND WHERE DO I FEEL IT IN MY BODY?

END OF MY DAY
WHAT EMOTION DO I FEEL AND WHERE DO I FEEL IT IN MY BODY?

INSIGHTS AND REFLECTIONS

3 THINGS I FEEL GRATEFUL TODAY ARE

_____
_____
_____

ONE MINUTE PRACTICE

Give yourself permission to tap on any point/s that feel comfortable for you whilst saying, 'I allow myself to be on a journey towards truth.'

NOTES

DATE:

BASIC RECIPE

EXPERIENCE/ ISSUE/ EVENT/ CHAKRA/ CHALLENGE I WANT TO WORK ON

EMOTIONS ATTACHED?
WHAT IS BENEATH THE EMOTION?

SET UP STATEMENT

SUDS

WHERE IS IT LOCATED IN THE BODY?
SCAN THE BODY. ANY SENSATIONS? TENSIONS? ETC.
COLOUR/ SIZE/ SHAPE/ TEMPERATURE/ TEXTURE/ WEIGHT/ SMELL/ TASTE?

AFFIRMATIONS AND CHOICES

INSIGHTS AND REFLECTIONS

OTHER EXPERIENCE/ ISSUE/ EVENT/ CHAKRA/ CHALLENGE THAT CAME THROUGH IN THE TAPPING ROUND?

DATE:

DAY 5

WAYS I INCORPORATED TAPPING INTO MY LIFE TODAY

- [ ] BASIC RECIPE
- [ ] PERSONAL PEACE PROCEDURE
- [ ] WITNESS TAPPING
- [ ] CHAKRA TAPPING
- [ ] SUBTLE TAPPING
- [ ] IMAGINAL TAPPING
- [ ] CONTINUAL TAPPING
- [ ] BORROWED BENEFITS

BEGINNING OF MY DAY
WHAT EMOTION DO I FEEL AND WHERE DO I FEEL IT IN MY BODY?

END OF MY DAY
WHAT EMOTION DO I FEEL AND WHERE DO I FEEL IT IN MY BODY?

INSIGHTS AND REFLECTIONS

3 THINGS I FEEL GRATEFUL TODAY ARE

_____
_____
_____

ONE MINUTE PRACTICE

Give yourself permission to tap on any point/s that feel comfortable for you whilst saying, 'In this present moment, I know I am enough.'

NOTES

DATE:

BASIC RECIPE

EXPERIENCE/ ISSUE/ EVENT/ CHAKRA/ CHALLENGE I WANT TO WORK ON

EMOTIONS ATTACHED?
WHAT IS BENEATH THE EMOTION?

SET UP STATEMENT

SUDS

WHERE IS IT LOCATED IN THE BODY?
SCAN THE BODY. ANY SENSATIONS? TENSIONS? ETC.
COLOUR/ SIZE/ SHAPE/ TEMPERATURE/ TEXTURE/ WEIGHT/ SMELL/ TASTE?

AFFIRMATIONS AND CHOICES

INSIGHTS AND REFLECTIONS

OTHER EXPERIENCE/ ISSUE/ EVENT/ CHAKRA/ CHALLENGE THAT CAME THROUGH IN THE TAPPING ROUND?

DATE:

DAY 6

WAYS I INCORPORATED TAPPING INTO MY LIFE TODAY

- [ ] BASIC RECIPE
- [ ] PERSONAL PEACE PROCEDURE
- [ ] WITNESS TAPPING
- [ ] CHAKRA TAPPING
- [ ] SUBTLE TAPPING
- [ ] IMAGINAL TAPPING
- [ ] CONTINUAL TAPPING
- [ ] BORROWED BENEFITS

BEGINNING OF MY DAY
WHAT EMOTION DO I FEEL AND WHERE DO I FEEL IT IN MY BODY?

END OF MY DAY
WHAT EMOTION DO I FEEL AND WHERE DO I FEEL IT IN MY BODY?

INSIGHTS AND REFLECTIONS

3 THINGS I FEEL GRATEFUL TODAY ARE

___

___

___

ONE MINUTE PRACTICE

Give yourself permission to tap on any point/s that feel comfortable for you whilst saying, 'I am worthy of healing and connection.'

NOTES

DATE:

BASIC RECIPE

EXPERIENCE/ ISSUE/ EVENT/ CHAKRA/ CHALLENGE I WANT TO WORK ON

EMOTIONS ATTACHED?
WHAT IS BENEATH THE EMOTION?

SET UP STATEMENT

SUDS

WHERE IS IT LOCATED IN THE BODY?
SCAN THE BODY. ANY SENSATIONS? TENSIONS? ETC.
COLOUR/ SIZE/ SHAPE/ TEMPERATURE/ TEXTURE/ WEIGHT/ SMELL/ TASTE?

AFFIRMATIONS AND CHOICES

INSIGHTS AND REFLECTIONS

OTHER EXPERIENCE/ ISSUE/ EVENT/ CHAKRA/ CHALLENGE THAT CAME THROUGH IN THE TAPPING ROUND?

DATE:

DAY 7

WAYS I INCORPORATED TAPPING INTO MY LIFE TODAY

- [ ] BASIC RECIPE
- [ ] PERSONAL PEACE PROCEDURE
- [ ] WITNESS TAPPING
- [ ] CHAKRA TAPPING
- [ ] SUBTLE TAPPING
- [ ] IMAGINAL TAPPING
- [ ] CONTINUAL TAPPING
- [ ] BORROWED BENEFITS

BEGINNING OF MY DAY
WHAT EMOTION DO I FEEL AND WHERE DO I FEEL IT IN MY BODY?

END OF MY DAY
WHAT EMOTION DO I FEEL AND WHERE DO I FEEL IT IN MY BODY?

INSIGHTS AND REFLECTIONS

3 THINGS I FEEL GRATEFUL TODAY ARE

_____
_____
_____

ONE MINUTE PRACTICE

Give yourself permission to tap on any point/s that feel comfortable for you whilst saying, 'I am allowed to choose me.'

NOTES

DATE:

BASIC RECIPE

EXPERIENCE/ ISSUE/ EVENT/ CHAKRA/ CHALLENGE I WANT TO WORK ON

EMOTIONS ATTACHED?
WHAT IS BENEATH THE EMOTION?

SET UP STATEMENT

SUDS

WHERE IS IT LOCATED IN THE BODY?
SCAN THE BODY. ANY SENSATIONS? TENSIONS? ETC.
COLOUR/ SIZE/ SHAPE/ TEMPERATURE/ TEXTURE/ WEIGHT/ SMELL/ TASTE?

AFFIRMATIONS AND CHOICES

INSIGHTS AND REFLECTIONS

OTHER EXPERIENCE/ ISSUE/ EVENT/ CHAKRA/ CHALLENGE THAT CAME THROUGH IN THE TAPPING ROUND?

DATE:

DAY 8

WAYS I INCORPORATED TAPPING INTO MY LIFE TODAY

- ☐ BASIC RECIPE
- ☐ PERSONAL PEACE PROCEDURE
- ☐ WITNESS TAPPING
- ☐ CHAKRA TAPPING
- ☐ SUBTLE TAPPING
- ☐ IMAGINAL TAPPING
- ☐ CONTINUAL TAPPING
- ☐ BORROWED BENEFITS

BEGINNING OF MY DAY
WHAT EMOTION DO I FEEL AND WHERE DO I FEEL IT IN MY BODY?

END OF MY DAY
WHAT EMOTION DO I FEEL AND WHERE DO I FEEL IT IN MY BODY?

INSIGHTS AND REFLECTIONS

3 THINGS I FEEL GRATEFUL TODAY ARE

___

___

___

ONE MINUTE PRACTICE

Give yourself permission to tap on any point/s that feel comfortable for you whilst saying, 'I release all my emotional attachments to surrendering to my shame as I allow myself to be seen.'

NOTES

DATE:

BASIC RECIPE

EXPERIENCE/ ISSUE/ EVENT/ CHAKRA/ CHALLENGE I WANT TO WORK ON

EMOTIONS ATTACHED?
WHAT IS BENEATH THE EMOTION?

SET UP STATEMENT

SUDS

WHERE IS IT LOCATED IN THE BODY?
SCAN THE BODY. ANY SENSATIONS? TENSIONS? ETC.
COLOUR/ SIZE/ SHAPE/ TEMPERATURE/ TEXTURE/ WEIGHT/ SMELL/ TASTE?

AFFIRMATIONS AND CHOICES

INSIGHTS AND REFLECTIONS

OTHER EXPERIENCE/ ISSUE/ EVENT/ CHAKRA/ CHALLENGE THAT CAME THROUGH IN THE TAPPING ROUND?

DATE:

DAY 9

WAYS I INCORPORATED TAPPING INTO MY LIFE TODAY

- [ ] BASIC RECIPE
- [ ] PERSONAL PEACE PROCEDURE
- [ ] WITNESS TAPPING
- [ ] CHAKRA TAPPING
- [ ] SUBTLE TAPPING
- [ ] IMAGINAL TAPPING
- [ ] CONTINUAL TAPPING
- [ ] BORROWED BENEFITS

BEGINNING OF MY DAY
WHAT EMOTION DO I FEEL AND WHERE DO I FEEL IT IN MY BODY?

END OF MY DAY
WHAT EMOTION DO I FEEL AND WHERE DO I FEEL IT IN MY BODY?

INSIGHTS AND REFLECTIONS

3 THINGS I FEEL GRATEFUL TODAY ARE

_____

_____

_____

ONE MINUTE PRACTICE

Give yourself permission to tap on any point/s that feel comfortable for you whilst saying, 'I give myself permission to be curious.'

NOTES

DATE:

BASIC RECIPE

EXPERIENCE/ ISSUE/ EVENT/ CHAKRA/ CHALLENGE I WANT TO WORK ON

EMOTIONS ATTACHED?
WHAT IS BENEATH THE EMOTION?

SET UP STATEMENT

SUDS

WHERE IS IT LOCATED IN THE BODY?
SCAN THE BODY. ANY SENSATIONS? TENSIONS? ETC.
COLOUR/ SIZE/ SHAPE/ TEMPERATURE/ TEXTURE/ WEIGHT/ SMELL/ TASTE?

AFFIRMATIONS AND CHOICES

INSIGHTS AND REFLECTIONS

OTHER EXPERIENCE/ ISSUE/ EVENT/ CHAKRA/ CHALLENGE THAT CAME THROUGH IN THE TAPPING ROUND?

DATE:

DAY 10

WAYS I INCORPORATED TAPPING INTO MY LIFE TODAY

- [ ] BASIC RECIPE
- [ ] PERSONAL PEACE PROCEDURE
- [ ] WITNESS TAPPING
- [ ] CHAKRA TAPPING
- [ ] SUBTLE TAPPING
- [ ] IMAGINAL TAPPING
- [ ] CONTINUAL TAPPING
- [ ] BORROWED BENEFITS

BEGINNING OF MY DAY
WHAT EMOTION DO I FEEL AND WHERE DO I FEEL IT IN MY BODY?

END OF MY DAY
WHAT EMOTION DO I FEEL AND WHERE DO I FEEL IT IN MY BODY?

INSIGHTS AND REFLECTIONS

3 THINGS I FEEL GRATEFUL TODAY ARE

_____

_____

_____

ONE MINUTE PRACTICE

Give yourself permission to tap on any point/s that feel comfortable for you whilst saying, 'I give myself permission to shine and take up space.'

NOTES

DATE:

BASIC RECIPE

EXPERIENCE/ ISSUE/ EVENT/ CHAKRA/ CHALLENGE I WANT TO WORK ON

EMOTIONS ATTACHED?
WHAT IS BENEATH THE EMOTION?

SET UP STATEMENT

SUDS

WHERE IS IT LOCATED IN THE BODY?
SCAN THE BODY. ANY SENSATIONS? TENSIONS? ETC.
COLOUR/ SIZE/ SHAPE/ TEMPERATURE/ TEXTURE/ WEIGHT/ SMELL/ TASTE?

AFFIRMATIONS AND CHOICES

INSIGHTS AND REFLECTIONS

OTHER EXPERIENCE/ ISSUE/ EVENT/ CHAKRA/ CHALLENGE THAT CAME THROUGH IN THE TAPPING ROUND?

DATE:

DAY 11

WAYS I INCORPORATED TAPPING INTO MY LIFE TODAY

- [ ] BASIC RECIPE
- [ ] PERSONAL PEACE PROCEDURE
- [ ] WITNESS TAPPING
- [ ] CHAKRA TAPPING
- [ ] SUBTLE TAPPING
- [ ] IMAGINAL TAPPING
- [ ] CONTINUAL TAPPING
- [ ] BORROWED BENEFITS

BEGINNING OF MY DAY
WHAT EMOTION DO I FEEL AND WHERE DO I FEEL IT IN MY BODY?

END OF MY DAY
WHAT EMOTION DO I FEEL AND WHERE DO I FEEL IT IN MY BODY?

INSIGHTS AND REFLECTIONS

3 THINGS I FEEL GRATEFUL TODAY ARE

_____
_____
_____

ONE MINUTE PRACTICE

Give yourself permission to tap on any point/s that feel comfortable for you whilst saying, 'I welcome opportunities for growth and expansion.'

NOTES

DATE:

BASIC RECIPE

EXPERIENCE/ ISSUE/ EVENT/ CHAKRA/ CHALLENGE I WANT TO WORK ON

EMOTIONS ATTACHED?
WHAT IS BENEATH THE EMOTION?

SET UP STATEMENT

SUDS

WHERE IS IT LOCATED IN THE BODY?
SCAN THE BODY. ANY SENSATIONS? TENSIONS? ETC.
COLOUR/ SIZE/ SHAPE/ TEMPERATURE/ TEXTURE/ WEIGHT/ SMELL/ TASTE?

AFFIRMATIONS AND CHOICES

INSIGHTS AND REFLECTIONS

OTHER EXPERIENCE/ ISSUE/ EVENT/ CHAKRA/ CHALLENGE THAT CAME THROUGH IN THE TAPPING ROUND?

DATE:

DAY 12

WAYS I INCORPORATED TAPPING INTO MY LIFE TODAY

- ☐ BASIC RECIPE
- ☐ PERSONAL PEACE PROCEDURE
- ☐ WITNESS TAPPING
- ☐ CHAKRA TAPPING
- ☐ SUBTLE TAPPING
- ☐ IMAGINAL TAPPING
- ☐ CONTINUAL TAPPING
- ☐ BORROWED BENEFITS

BEGINNING OF MY DAY
WHAT EMOTION DO I FEEL AND WHERE DO I FEEL IT IN MY BODY?

END OF MY DAY
WHAT EMOTION DO I FEEL AND WHERE DO I FEEL IT IN MY BODY?

INSIGHTS AND REFLECTIONS

3 THINGS I FEEL GRATEFUL TODAY ARE

_____
_____
_____

ONE MINUTE PRACTICE

Give yourself permission to tap on any point/s that feel comfortable for you whilst saying, 'I choose to release what no longer resonates to make room for new possibilities.'

NOTES

DATE:

BASIC RECIPE

EXPERIENCE/ ISSUE/ EVENT/ CHAKRA/ CHALLENGE I WANT TO WORK ON

EMOTIONS ATTACHED?
WHAT IS BENEATH THE EMOTION?

SET UP STATEMENT

SUDS

WHERE IS IT LOCATED IN THE BODY?
SCAN THE BODY. ANY SENSATIONS? TENSIONS? ETC.
COLOUR/ SIZE/ SHAPE/ TEMPERATURE/ TEXTURE/ WEIGHT/ SMELL/ TASTE?

AFFIRMATIONS AND CHOICES

INSIGHTS AND REFLECTIONS

OTHER EXPERIENCE/ ISSUE/ EVENT/ CHAKRA/ CHALLENGE THAT CAME THROUGH IN THE TAPPING ROUND?

DATE:

DAY 13

WAYS I INCORPORATED TAPPING INTO MY LIFE TODAY

- [ ] BASIC RECIPE
- [ ] PERSONAL PEACE PROCEDURE
- [ ] WITNESS TAPPING
- [ ] CHAKRA TAPPING
- [ ] SUBTLE TAPPING
- [ ] IMAGINAL TAPPING
- [ ] CONTINUAL TAPPING
- [ ] BORROWED BENEFITS

BEGINNING OF MY DAY
WHAT EMOTION DO I FEEL AND WHERE DO I FEEL IT IN MY BODY?

END OF MY DAY
WHAT EMOTION DO I FEEL AND WHERE DO I FEEL IT IN MY BODY?

INSIGHTS AND REFLECTIONS

3 THINGS I FEEL GRATEFUL TODAY ARE

_____
_____
_____

ONE MINUTE PRACTICE

Give yourself permission to tap on any point/s that feel comfortable for you whilst saying, 'I choose to breathe in confidence and breathe out fear.'

NOTES

DATE:

BASIC RECIPE

EXPERIENCE/ ISSUE/ EVENT/ CHAKRA/ CHALLENGE I WANT TO WORK ON

EMOTIONS ATTACHED?
WHAT IS BENEATH THE EMOTION?

SET UP STATEMENT

SUDS

WHERE IS IT LOCATED IN THE BODY?
SCAN THE BODY. ANY SENSATIONS? TENSIONS? ETC.
COLOUR/ SIZE/ SHAPE/ TEMPERATURE/ TEXTURE/ WEIGHT/ SMELL/ TASTE?

AFFIRMATIONS AND CHOICES

INSIGHTS AND REFLECTIONS

OTHER EXPERIENCE/ ISSUE/ EVENT/ CHAKRA/ CHALLENGE THAT CAME THROUGH IN THE TAPPING ROUND?

DATE:

DAY 14

WAYS I INCORPORATED TAPPING INTO MY LIFE TODAY

- ☐ BASIC RECIPE
- ☐ PERSONAL PEACE PROCEDURE
- ☐ WITNESS TAPPING
- ☐ CHAKRA TAPPING
- ☐ SUBTLE TAPPING
- ☐ IMAGINAL TAPPING
- ☐ CONTINUAL TAPPING
- ☐ BORROWED BENEFITS

BEGINNING OF MY DAY
WHAT EMOTION DO I FEEL AND WHERE DO I FEEL IT IN MY BODY?

END OF MY DAY
WHAT EMOTION DO I FEEL AND WHERE DO I FEEL IT IN MY BODY?

INSIGHTS AND REFLECTIONS

3 THINGS I FEEL GRATEFUL TODAY ARE

_____
_____
_____

ONE MINUTE PRACTICE

Give yourself permission to tap on any point/s that feel comfortable for you whilst saying, 'I release all my emotional attachments with my need to be perfect.'

NOTES

DATE:

BASIC RECIPE

EXPERIENCE/ ISSUE/ EVENT/ CHAKRA/ CHALLENGE I WANT TO WORK ON

EMOTIONS ATTACHED?
WHAT IS BENEATH THE EMOTION?

SET UP STATEMENT

SUDS

WHERE IS IT LOCATED IN THE BODY?
SCAN THE BODY. ANY SENSATIONS? TENSIONS? ETC.
COLOUR/ SIZE/ SHAPE/ TEMPERATURE/ TEXTURE/ WEIGHT/ SMELL/ TASTE?

AFFIRMATIONS AND CHOICES

INSIGHTS AND REFLECTIONS

OTHER EXPERIENCE/ ISSUE/ EVENT/ CHAKRA/ CHALLENGE THAT CAME THROUGH IN THE TAPPING ROUND?

DATE:

DAY 15

WAYS I INCORPORATED TAPPING INTO MY LIFE TODAY

- [ ] BASIC RECIPE
- [ ] PERSONAL PEACE PROCEDURE
- [ ] WITNESS TAPPING
- [ ] CHAKRA TAPPING
- [ ] SUBTLE TAPPING
- [ ] IMAGINAL TAPPING
- [ ] CONTINUAL TAPPING
- [ ] BORROWED BENEFITS

BEGINNING OF MY DAY
WHAT EMOTION DO I FEEL AND WHERE DO I FEEL IT IN MY BODY?

END OF MY DAY
WHAT EMOTION DO I FEEL AND WHERE DO I FEEL IT IN MY BODY?

INSIGHTS AND REFLECTIONS

3 THINGS I FEEL GRATEFUL TODAY ARE

_____
_____
_____

ONE MINUTE PRACTICE

Give yourself permission to tap on any point/s that feel comfortable for you whilst saying, 'I choose to take up space.'

NOTES

DATE:

BASIC RECIPE

EXPERIENCE/ ISSUE/ EVENT/ CHAKRA/ CHALLENGE I WANT TO WORK ON

EMOTIONS ATTACHED?
WHAT IS BENEATH THE EMOTION?

SET UP STATEMENT

SUDS

WHERE IS IT LOCATED IN THE BODY?
SCAN THE BODY. ANY SENSATIONS? TENSIONS? ETC.
COLOUR/ SIZE/ SHAPE/ TEMPERATURE/ TEXTURE/ WEIGHT/ SMELL/ TASTE?

AFFIRMATIONS AND CHOICES

INSIGHTS AND REFLECTIONS

OTHER EXPERIENCE/ ISSUE/ EVENT/ CHAKRA/ CHALLENGE THAT CAME THROUGH IN THE TAPPING ROUND?

DATE:

DAY 16

WAYS I INCORPORATED TAPPING INTO MY LIFE TODAY

- [ ] BASIC RECIPE
- [ ] PERSONAL PEACE PROCEDURE
- [ ] WITNESS TAPPING
- [ ] CHAKRA TAPPING
- [ ] SUBTLE TAPPING
- [ ] IMAGINAL TAPPING
- [ ] CONTINUAL TAPPING
- [ ] BORROWED BENEFITS

BEGINNING OF MY DAY
WHAT EMOTION DO I FEEL AND WHERE DO I FEEL IT IN MY BODY?

END OF MY DAY
WHAT EMOTION DO I FEEL AND WHERE DO I FEEL IT IN MY BODY?

INSIGHTS AND REFLECTIONS

3 THINGS I FEEL GRATEFUL TODAY ARE

_____
_____
_____

ONE MINUTE PRACTICE

Give yourself permission to tap on any point/s that feel comfortable for you whilst saying, 'I honor the distances I have travelled to meet myself.'

NOTES

DATE:

BASIC RECIPE

EXPERIENCE/ ISSUE/ EVENT/ CHAKRA/ CHALLENGE I WANT TO WORK ON

EMOTIONS ATTACHED?
WHAT IS BENEATH THE EMOTION?

SET UP STATEMENT

SUDS

WHERE IS IT LOCATED IN THE BODY?
SCAN THE BODY. ANY SENSATIONS? TENSIONS? ETC.
COLOUR/ SIZE/ SHAPE/ TEMPERATURE/ TEXTURE/ WEIGHT/ SMELL/ TASTE?

AFFIRMATIONS AND CHOICES

INSIGHTS AND REFLECTIONS

OTHER EXPERIENCE/ ISSUE/ EVENT/ CHAKRA/ CHALLENGE THAT CAME THROUGH IN THE TAPPING ROUND?

DATE:

DAY 17

WAYS I INCORPORATED TAPPING INTO MY LIFE TODAY

- ☐ BASIC RECIPE
- ☐ PERSONAL PEACE PROCEDURE
- ☐ WITNESS TAPPING
- ☐ CHAKRA TAPPING
- ☐ SUBTLE TAPPING
- ☐ IMAGINAL TAPPING
- ☐ CONTINUAL TAPPING
- ☐ BORROWED BENEFITS

BEGINNING OF MY DAY
WHAT EMOTION DO I FEEL AND WHERE DO I FEEL IT IN MY BODY?

END OF MY DAY
WHAT EMOTION DO I FEEL AND WHERE DO I FEEL IT IN MY BODY?

INSIGHTS AND REFLECTIONS

3 THINGS I FEEL GRATEFUL TODAY ARE

_____
_____
_____

ONE MINUTE PRACTICE

Give yourself permission to tap on any point/s that feel comfortable for you whilst saying, 'I choose to release the expectations others have of me.'

NOTES

DATE:

BASIC RECIPE

EXPERIENCE/ ISSUE/ EVENT/ CHAKRA/ CHALLENGE I WANT TO WORK ON

EMOTIONS ATTACHED?
WHAT IS BENEATH THE EMOTION?

SET UP STATEMENT

SUDS

WHERE IS IT LOCATED IN THE BODY?
SCAN THE BODY. ANY SENSATIONS? TENSIONS? ETC.
COLOUR/ SIZE/ SHAPE/ TEMPERATURE/ TEXTURE/ WEIGHT/ SMELL/ TASTE?

AFFIRMATIONS AND CHOICES

INSIGHTS AND REFLECTIONS

OTHER EXPERIENCE/ ISSUE/ EVENT/ CHAKRA/ CHALLENGE THAT CAME THROUGH IN THE TAPPING ROUND?

DATE:

DAY 18

WAYS I INCORPORATED TAPPING INTO MY LIFE TODAY

- ☐ BASIC RECIPE
- ☐ PERSONAL PEACE PROCEDURE
- ☐ WITNESS TAPPING
- ☐ CHAKRA TAPPING

- ☐ SUBTLE TAPPING
- ☐ IMAGINAL TAPPING
- ☐ CONTINUAL TAPPING
- ☐ BORROWED BENEFITS

BEGINNING OF MY DAY
WHAT EMOTION DO I FEEL AND WHERE DO I FEEL IT IN MY BODY?

END OF MY DAY
WHAT EMOTION DO I FEEL AND WHERE DO I FEEL IT IN MY BODY?

INSIGHTS AND REFLECTIONS

3 THINGS I FEEL GRATEFUL TODAY ARE

_____
_____
_____

ONE MINUTE PRACTICE

Give yourself permission to tap on any point/s that feel comfortable for you whilst saying, 'I am brave enough to try.'

NOTES

DATE:

BASIC RECIPE

EXPERIENCE/ ISSUE/ EVENT/ CHAKRA/ CHALLENGE I WANT TO WORK ON

EMOTIONS ATTACHED?
WHAT IS BENEATH THE EMOTION?

SET UP STATEMENT

SUDS

WHERE IS IT LOCATED IN THE BODY?
SCAN THE BODY. ANY SENSATIONS? TENSIONS? ETC.
COLOUR/ SIZE/ SHAPE/ TEMPERATURE/ TEXTURE/ WEIGHT/ SMELL/ TASTE?

AFFIRMATIONS AND CHOICES

INSIGHTS AND REFLECTIONS

OTHER EXPERIENCE/ ISSUE/ EVENT/ CHAKRA/ CHALLENGE THAT CAME THROUGH IN THE TAPPING ROUND?

DATE:

DAY 19

WAYS I INCORPORATED TAPPING INTO MY LIFE TODAY

- ☐ BASIC RECIPE
- ☐ PERSONAL PEACE PROCEDURE
- ☐ WITNESS TAPPING
- ☐ CHAKRA TAPPING
- ☐ SUBTLE TAPPING
- ☐ IMAGINAL TAPPING
- ☐ CONTINUAL TAPPING
- ☐ BORROWED BENEFITS

BEGINNING OF MY DAY
WHAT EMOTION DO I FEEL AND WHERE DO I FEEL IT IN MY BODY?

END OF MY DAY
WHAT EMOTION DO I FEEL AND WHERE DO I FEEL IT IN MY BODY?

INSIGHTS AND REFLECTIONS

3 THINGS I FEEL GRATEFUL TODAY ARE

_____
_____
_____

ONE MINUTE PRACTICE

Give yourself permission to tap on any point/s that feel comfortable for you whilst saying, 'Today I believe in me.'

NOTES

DATE:

BASIC RECIPE

EXPERIENCE/ ISSUE/ EVENT/ CHAKRA/ CHALLENGE I WANT TO WORK ON

**EMOTIONS ATTACHED?
WHAT IS BENEATH THE EMOTION?**

SET UP STATEMENT

SUDS

**WHERE IS IT LOCATED IN THE BODY?
SCAN THE BODY. ANY SENSATIONS? TENSIONS? ETC.
COLOUR/ SIZE/ SHAPE/ TEMPERATURE/ TEXTURE/ WEIGHT/ SMELL/ TASTE?**

AFFIRMATIONS AND CHOICES

INSIGHTS AND REFLECTIONS

OTHER EXPERIENCE/ ISSUE/ EVENT/ CHAKRA/ CHALLENGE THAT CAME THROUGH IN THE TAPPING ROUND?

DATE:

DAY 20

WAYS I INCORPORATED TAPPING INTO MY LIFE TODAY

- [ ] BASIC RECIPE
- [ ] PERSONAL PEACE PROCEDURE
- [ ] WITNESS TAPPING
- [ ] CHAKRA TAPPING
- [ ] SUBTLE TAPPING
- [ ] IMAGINAL TAPPING
- [ ] CONTINUAL TAPPING
- [ ] BORROWED BENEFITS

BEGINNING OF MY DAY
WHAT EMOTION DO I FEEL AND WHERE DO I FEEL IT IN MY BODY?

END OF MY DAY
WHAT EMOTION DO I FEEL AND WHERE DO I FEEL IT IN MY BODY?

INSIGHTS AND REFLECTIONS

3 THINGS I FEEL GRATEFUL TODAY ARE

_____
_____
_____

ONE MINUTE PRACTICE

Give yourself permission to tap on any point/s that feel comfortable for you whilst saying, 'I allow myself time and space when I need it.'

NOTES

DATE:

BASIC RECIPE

EXPERIENCE/ ISSUE/ EVENT/ CHAKRA/ CHALLENGE I WANT TO WORK ON

EMOTIONS ATTACHED?
WHAT IS BENEATH THE EMOTION?

SET UP STATEMENT

SUDS

WHERE IS IT LOCATED IN THE BODY?
SCAN THE BODY. ANY SENSATIONS? TENSIONS? ETC.
COLOUR/ SIZE/ SHAPE/ TEMPERATURE/ TEXTURE/ WEIGHT/ SMELL/ TASTE?

AFFIRMATIONS AND CHOICES

INSIGHTS AND REFLECTIONS

OTHER EXPERIENCE/ ISSUE/ EVENT/ CHAKRA/ CHALLENGE THAT CAME THROUGH IN THE TAPPING ROUND?

DATE:

DAY 21

WAYS I INCORPORATED TAPPING INTO MY LIFE TODAY

- [ ] BASIC RECIPE
- [ ] PERSONAL PEACE PROCEDURE
- [ ] WITNESS TAPPING
- [ ] CHAKRA TAPPING
- [ ] SUBTLE TAPPING
- [ ] IMAGINAL TAPPING
- [ ] CONTINUAL TAPPING
- [ ] BORROWED BENEFITS

BEGINNING OF MY DAY
WHAT EMOTION DO I FEEL AND WHERE DO I FEEL IT IN MY BODY?

END OF MY DAY
WHAT EMOTION DO I FEEL AND WHERE DO I FEEL IT IN MY BODY?

INSIGHTS AND REFLECTIONS

3 THINGS I FEEL GRATEFUL TODAY ARE

_____
_____
_____

ONE MINUTE PRACTICE

Give yourself permission to tap on any point/s that feel comfortable for you whilst saying, 'I am worthy of support and compassion.'

NOTES

DATE:

BASIC RECIPE

EXPERIENCE/ ISSUE/ EVENT/ CHAKRA/ CHALLENGE I WANT TO WORK ON

EMOTIONS ATTACHED?
WHAT IS BENEATH THE EMOTION?

SET UP STATEMENT

SUDS

WHERE IS IT LOCATED IN THE BODY?
SCAN THE BODY. ANY SENSATIONS? TENSIONS? ETC.
COLOUR/ SIZE/ SHAPE/ TEMPERATURE/ TEXTURE/ WEIGHT/ SMELL/ TASTE?

AFFIRMATIONS AND CHOICES

INSIGHTS AND REFLECTIONS

OTHER EXPERIENCE/ ISSUE/ EVENT/ CHAKRA/ CHALLENGE THAT CAME THROUGH IN THE TAPPING ROUND?

DATE:

DAY 22

WAYS I INCORPORATED TAPPING INTO MY LIFE TODAY

- [ ] BASIC RECIPE
- [ ] PERSONAL PEACE PROCEDURE
- [ ] WITNESS TAPPING
- [ ] CHAKRA TAPPING
- [ ] SUBTLE TAPPING
- [ ] IMAGINAL TAPPING
- [ ] CONTINUAL TAPPING
- [ ] BORROWED BENEFITS

BEGINNING OF MY DAY
WHAT EMOTION DO I FEEL AND WHERE DO I FEEL IT IN MY BODY?

END OF MY DAY
WHAT EMOTION DO I FEEL AND WHERE DO I FEEL IT IN MY BODY?

INSIGHTS AND REFLECTIONS

3 THINGS I FEEL GRATEFUL TODAY ARE

_____
_____
_____

ONE MINUTE PRACTICE

Give yourself permission to tap on any point/s that feel comfortable for you whilst saying, 'I give myself permission to feel.'

NOTES

DATE:

BASIC RECIPE

EXPERIENCE/ ISSUE/ EVENT/ CHAKRA/ CHALLENGE I WANT TO WORK ON

EMOTIONS ATTACHED?
WHAT IS BENEATH THE EMOTION?

SET UP STATEMENT

SUDS

WHERE IS IT LOCATED IN THE BODY?
SCAN THE BODY. ANY SENSATIONS? TENSIONS? ETC.
COLOUR/ SIZE/ SHAPE/ TEMPERATURE/ TEXTURE/ WEIGHT/ SMELL/ TASTE?

AFFIRMATIONS AND CHOICES

INSIGHTS AND REFLECTIONS

OTHER EXPERIENCE/ ISSUE/ EVENT/ CHAKRA/ CHALLENGE THAT CAME THROUGH IN THE TAPPING ROUND?

DATE:

DAY 23

WAYS I INCORPORATED TAPPING INTO MY LIFE TODAY

- [ ] BASIC RECIPE
- [ ] PERSONAL PEACE PROCEDURE
- [ ] WITNESS TAPPING
- [ ] CHAKRA TAPPING
- [ ] SUBTLE TAPPING
- [ ] IMAGINAL TAPPING
- [ ] CONTINUAL TAPPING
- [ ] BORROWED BENEFITS

BEGINNING OF MY DAY
WHAT EMOTION DO I FEEL AND WHERE DO I FEEL IT IN MY BODY?

END OF MY DAY
WHAT EMOTION DO I FEEL AND WHERE DO I FEEL IT IN MY BODY?

INSIGHTS AND REFLECTIONS

3 THINGS I FEEL GRATEFUL TODAY ARE

_____
_____
_____

ONE MINUTE PRACTICE

Give yourself permission to tap on any point/s that feel comfortable for you whilst saying, 'I choose to break free from my limiting beliefs.'

NOTES

DATE:

BASIC RECIPE

EXPERIENCE/ ISSUE/ EVENT/ CHAKRA/ CHALLENGE I WANT TO WORK ON

EMOTIONS ATTACHED?
WHAT IS BENEATH THE EMOTION?

SET UP STATEMENT

SUDS

WHERE IS IT LOCATED IN THE BODY?
SCAN THE BODY. ANY SENSATIONS? TENSIONS? ETC.
COLOUR/ SIZE/ SHAPE/ TEMPERATURE/ TEXTURE/ WEIGHT/ SMELL/ TASTE?

AFFIRMATIONS AND CHOICES

INSIGHTS AND REFLECTIONS

OTHER EXPERIENCE/ ISSUE/ EVENT/ CHAKRA/ CHALLENGE THAT CAME THROUGH IN THE TAPPING ROUND?

DATE:

DAY 24

WAYS I INCORPORATED TAPPING INTO MY LIFE TODAY

- [ ] BASIC RECIPE
- [ ] PERSONAL PEACE PROCEDURE
- [ ] WITNESS TAPPING
- [ ] CHAKRA TAPPING
- [ ] SUBTLE TAPPING
- [ ] IMAGINAL TAPPING
- [ ] CONTINUAL TAPPING
- [ ] BORROWED BENEFITS

BEGINNING OF MY DAY
WHAT EMOTION DO I FEEL AND WHERE DO I FEEL IT IN MY BODY?

END OF MY DAY
WHAT EMOTION DO I FEEL AND WHERE DO I FEEL IT IN MY BODY?

INSIGHTS AND REFLECTIONS

3 THINGS I FEEL GRATEFUL TODAY ARE

_____
_____
_____

ONE MINUTE PRACTICE

Give yourself permission to tap on any point/s that feel comfortable for you whilst saying, 'I am enough just being myself.'

NOTES

DATE:

BASIC RECIPE

EXPERIENCE/ ISSUE/ EVENT/ CHAKRA/ CHALLENGE I WANT TO WORK ON

EMOTIONS ATTACHED?
WHAT IS BENEATH THE EMOTION?

SET UP STATEMENT

SUDS

WHERE IS IT LOCATED IN THE BODY?
SCAN THE BODY. ANY SENSATIONS? TENSIONS? ETC.
COLOUR/ SIZE/ SHAPE/ TEMPERATURE/ TEXTURE/ WEIGHT/ SMELL/ TASTE?

AFFIRMATIONS AND CHOICES

INSIGHTS AND REFLECTIONS

OTHER EXPERIENCE/ ISSUE/ EVENT/ CHAKRA/ CHALLENGE THAT CAME THROUGH IN THE TAPPING ROUND?

DATE:

DAY 25

WAYS I INCORPORATED TAPPING INTO MY LIFE TODAY

- [ ] BASIC RECIPE
- [ ] PERSONAL PEACE PROCEDURE
- [ ] WITNESS TAPPING
- [ ] CHAKRA TAPPING
- [ ] SUBTLE TAPPING
- [ ] IMAGINAL TAPPING
- [ ] CONTINUAL TAPPING
- [ ] BORROWED BENEFITS

BEGINNING OF MY DAY
WHAT EMOTION DO I FEEL AND WHERE DO I FEEL IT IN MY BODY?

END OF MY DAY
WHAT EMOTION DO I FEEL AND WHERE DO I FEEL IT IN MY BODY?

INSIGHTS AND REFLECTIONS

3 THINGS I FEEL GRATEFUL TODAY ARE

_____
_____
_____

ONE MINUTE PRACTICE

Give yourself permission to tap on any point/s that feel comfortable for you whilst saying, 'I allow energy to shift, to make room, to make room for what I need now.'

NOTES

DATE:

BASIC RECIPE

EXPERIENCE/ ISSUE/ EVENT/ CHAKRA/ CHALLENGE I WANT TO WORK ON

EMOTIONS ATTACHED? WHAT IS BENEATH THE EMOTION?

SET UP STATEMENT

SUDS

WHERE IS IT LOCATED IN THE BODY? SCAN THE BODY. ANY SENSATIONS? TENSIONS? ETC. COLOUR/ SIZE/ SHAPE/ TEMPERATURE/ TEXTURE/ WEIGHT/ SMELL/ TASTE?

AFFIRMATIONS AND CHOICES

INSIGHTS AND REFLECTIONS

OTHER EXPERIENCE/ ISSUE/ EVENT/ CHAKRA/ CHALLENGE THAT CAME THROUGH IN THE TAPPING ROUND?

DATE:

DAY 26

WAYS I INCORPORATED TAPPING INTO MY LIFE TODAY

- [ ] BASIC RECIPE
- [ ] PERSONAL PEACE PROCEDURE
- [ ] WITNESS TAPPING
- [ ] CHAKRA TAPPING
- [ ] SUBTLE TAPPING
- [ ] IMAGINAL TAPPING
- [ ] CONTINUAL TAPPING
- [ ] BORROWED BENEFITS

BEGINNING OF MY DAY
WHAT EMOTION DO I FEEL AND WHERE DO I FEEL IT IN MY BODY?

END OF MY DAY
WHAT EMOTION DO I FEEL AND WHERE DO I FEEL IT IN MY BODY?

INSIGHTS AND REFLECTIONS

3 THINGS I FEEL GRATEFUL TODAY ARE

_____
_____
_____

ONE MINUTE PRACTICE

Give yourself permission to tap on any point/s that feel comfortable for you whilst saying, 'I allow my heart to open to new truths.'

NOTES

DATE:

BASIC RECIPE

EXPERIENCE/ ISSUE/ EVENT/ CHAKRA/
CHALLENGE I WANT TO WORK ON

EMOTIONS ATTACHED?
WHAT IS BENEATH THE EMOTION?

SET UP STATEMENT

SUDS

WHERE IS IT LOCATED IN THE BODY?
SCAN THE BODY. ANY SENSATIONS? TENSIONS? ETC.
COLOUR/ SIZE/ SHAPE/ TEMPERATURE/ TEXTURE/ WEIGHT/ SMELL/ TASTE?

AFFIRMATIONS AND CHOICES

INSIGHTS AND REFLECTIONS

OTHER EXPERIENCE/ ISSUE/ EVENT/ CHAKRA/ CHALLENGE THAT CAME THROUGH IN THE TAPPING ROUND?

DATE:

DAY 27

WAYS I INCORPORATED TAPPING INTO MY LIFE TODAY

- [ ] BASIC RECIPE
- [ ] PERSONAL PEACE PROCEDURE
- [ ] WITNESS TAPPING
- [ ] CHAKRA TAPPING
- [ ] SUBTLE TAPPING
- [ ] IMAGINAL TAPPING
- [ ] CONTINUAL TAPPING
- [ ] BORROWED BENEFITS

BEGINNING OF MY DAY
WHAT EMOTION DO I FEEL AND WHERE DO I FEEL IT IN MY BODY?

END OF MY DAY
WHAT EMOTION DO I FEEL AND WHERE DO I FEEL IT IN MY BODY?

INSIGHTS AND REFLECTIONS

3 THINGS I FEEL GRATEFUL TODAY ARE

_____
_____
_____

ONE MINUTE PRACTICE

Give yourself permission to tap on any point/s that feel comfortable for you whilst saying, 'My emotional needs are valid.'

NOTES

DATE:

BASIC RECIPE

EXPERIENCE/ ISSUE/ EVENT/ CHAKRA/ CHALLENGE I WANT TO WORK ON

EMOTIONS ATTACHED?
WHAT IS BENEATH THE EMOTION?

SET UP STATEMENT

SUDS

WHERE IS IT LOCATED IN THE BODY?
SCAN THE BODY. ANY SENSATIONS? TENSIONS? ETC.
COLOUR/ SIZE/ SHAPE/ TEMPERATURE/ TEXTURE/ WEIGHT/ SMELL/ TASTE?

AFFIRMATIONS AND CHOICES

INSIGHTS AND REFLECTIONS

OTHER EXPERIENCE/ ISSUE/ EVENT/ CHAKRA/ CHALLENGE THAT CAME THROUGH IN THE TAPPING ROUND?

DATE:

DAY 28

WAYS I INCORPORATED TAPPING INTO MY LIFE TODAY

- [ ] BASIC RECIPE
- [ ] PERSONAL PEACE PROCEDURE
- [ ] WITNESS TAPPING
- [ ] CHAKRA TAPPING
- [ ] SUBTLE TAPPING
- [ ] IMAGINAL TAPPING
- [ ] CONTINUAL TAPPING
- [ ] BORROWED BENEFITS

BEGINNING OF MY DAY
WHAT EMOTION DO I FEEL AND WHERE DO I FEEL IT IN MY BODY?

END OF MY DAY
WHAT EMOTION DO I FEEL AND WHERE DO I FEEL IT IN MY BODY?

INSIGHTS AND REFLECTIONS

3 THINGS I FEEL GRATEFUL TODAY ARE

_____
_____
_____

ONE MINUTE PRACTICE

Give yourself permission to tap on any point/s that feel comfortable for you whilst saying, 'I choose to create more simplicity and peacefulness in my life.'

NOTES

DATE:

BASIC RECIPE

EXPERIENCE/ ISSUE/ EVENT/ CHAKRA/ CHALLENGE I WANT TO WORK ON

EMOTIONS ATTACHED?
WHAT IS BENEATH THE EMOTION?

SET UP STATEMENT

SUDS

WHERE IS IT LOCATED IN THE BODY?
SCAN THE BODY. ANY SENSATIONS? TENSIONS? ETC.
COLOUR/ SIZE/ SHAPE/ TEMPERATURE/ TEXTURE/ WEIGHT/ SMELL/ TASTE?

AFFIRMATIONS AND CHOICES

INSIGHTS AND REFLECTIONS

OTHER EXPERIENCE/ ISSUE/ EVENT/ CHAKRA/ CHALLENGE THAT CAME THROUGH IN THE TAPPING ROUND?

DATE:

DAY 29

WAYS I INCORPORATED TAPPING INTO MY LIFE TODAY

- [ ] BASIC RECIPE
- [ ] PERSONAL PEACE PROCEDURE
- [ ] WITNESS TAPPING
- [ ] CHAKRA TAPPING
- [ ] SUBTLE TAPPING
- [ ] IMAGINAL TAPPING
- [ ] CONTINUAL TAPPING
- [ ] BORROWED BENEFITS

BEGINNING OF MY DAY
WHAT EMOTION DO I FEEL AND WHERE DO I FEEL IT IN MY BODY?

END OF MY DAY
WHAT EMOTION DO I FEEL AND WHERE DO I FEEL IT IN MY BODY?

INSIGHTS AND REFLECTIONS

3 THINGS I FEEL GRATEFUL TODAY ARE

_____
_____
_____

ONE MINUTE PRACTICE

Give yourself permission to tap on any point/s that feel comfortable for you whilst saying, 'I am whole, I am valid, and I exist.'

NOTES

DATE:

BASIC RECIPE

EXPERIENCE/ ISSUE/ EVENT/ CHAKRA/
CHALLENGE I WANT TO WORK ON

EMOTIONS ATTACHED?
WHAT IS BENEATH THE EMOTION?

SET UP STATEMENT

SUDS

WHERE IS IT LOCATED IN THE BODY?
SCAN THE BODY. ANY SENSATIONS? TENSIONS? ETC.
COLOUR/ SIZE/ SHAPE/ TEMPERATURE/ TEXTURE/ WEIGHT/ SMELL/ TASTE?

AFFIRMATIONS AND CHOICES

INSIGHTS AND REFLECTIONS

OTHER EXPERIENCE/ ISSUE/ EVENT/ CHAKRA/ CHALLENGE THAT CAME THROUGH IN THE TAPPING ROUND?

DATE:

DAY 30

WAYS I INCORPORATED TAPPING INTO MY LIFE TODAY

- [ ] BASIC RECIPE
- [ ] PERSONAL PEACE PROCEDURE
- [ ] WITNESS TAPPING
- [ ] CHAKRA TAPPING

- [ ] SUBTLE TAPPING
- [ ] IMAGINAL TAPPING
- [ ] CONTINUAL TAPPING
- [ ] BORROWED BENEFITS

BEGINNING OF MY DAY
WHAT EMOTION DO I FEEL AND WHERE DO I FEEL IT IN MY BODY?

END OF MY DAY
WHAT EMOTION DO I FEEL AND WHERE DO I FEEL IT IN MY BODY?

INSIGHTS AND REFLECTIONS

3 THINGS I FEEL GRATEFUL TODAY ARE

_____
_____
_____

ONE MINUTE PRACTICE

Give yourself permission to tap on any point/s that feel comfortable for you whilst saying, 'I am grateful for my journey and where I am now.'

NOTES

DATE:

BASIC RECIPE

EXPERIENCE/ ISSUE/ EVENT/ CHAKRA/ CHALLENGE I WANT TO WORK ON

EMOTIONS ATTACHED?
WHAT IS BENEATH THE EMOTION?

SET UP STATEMENT

SUDS

WHERE IS IT LOCATED IN THE BODY?
SCAN THE BODY. ANY SENSATIONS? TENSIONS? ETC.
COLOUR/ SIZE/ SHAPE/ TEMPERATURE/ TEXTURE/ WEIGHT/ SMELL/ TASTE?

AFFIRMATIONS AND CHOICES

INSIGHTS AND REFLECTIONS

OTHER EXPERIENCE/ ISSUE/ EVENT/ CHAKRA/ CHALLENGE THAT CAME THROUGH IN THE TAPPING ROUND?

Chapter Eight

Tapping Scripts

TAPPING SCRIPTS

Write down any tapping scripts you have created for yourself so you can come back and continue tapping on it.

_____

_____

_____

_____

_____

_____

_____

_____

_____

_____

_____

_____

_____

_____

_____

_____

_____

TAPPING SCRIPTS

TAPPING SCRIPTS

TAPPING SCRIPTS

TAPPING SCRIPTS

Chapter Nine

Reflection and Notes

REFLECTIONS

Invite yourself time to answer these questions with honesty to yourself.

How was your journey with incorporating the practices in this book?

_____

_____

_____

_____

_____

_____

What resistance, if any, did you have with this workbook?

_____

_____

_____

_____

_____

_____

What has completing this workbook revealed to you?

_____
_____
_____
_____
_____
_____
_____

How will you will continue to incorporate EFT and other tapping practices into your life?

_____
_____
_____
_____
_____
_____
_____
_____
_____

NOTES

NOTES

NOTES

NOTES

Thank You

Thank you for allowing me to be a part of your support system with my workbook. This workbook, along with the Foundations of Tapping: Inviting EFT and Other Tapping Practices into Your Life book was designed to support you in your healing journey. I hope it has supported you. Healing journeys are cyclical in nature, so please know you can always come back to this workbook and the Foundations of Tapping: Inviting EFT and Other Tapping Practices into Your Life book at any time throughout your life.

Tapping is a great tool to do by yourself, and I hope by reading and participating in the practices, you were able to incorporate tapping into your life. Although you can do tapping by yourself, it doesn't mean you must only do it by yourself. If anything is overwhelming your system, know you can have extra support and guidance with an appropriate practitioner.

Embarking on your healing journey is a journey of discovering yourself. Please know you may have completed this workbook, but it doesn't mean you need to finish inviting tapping into your life. Know you can always do this workbook again and continue incorporating these practices into your life.

All my love,

Stacey

About the Author

Stacey Webb is an award-winning author, Intuitive Somatic Mentor, Trauma-Trained Somatic Practitioner, and Warrior of Grace, who resides in Australia with her husband and four children.

During Stacey's 16-year career as a Detective within the Police Force, Stacey studied on trauma, the nervous system, and obtained many certifications and qualifications in EFT and other tapping practices, breathwork, somatic therapy, embodiment, and intuitive intelligence to support people on their healing journey as they; release trauma, stored emotions, energy blocks, and limiting beliefs that may create limitations in one's life.

Stacey is also the author of 'The Intuitive Detective,' which has received amazing reviews from readers all over the world, and has won multiple book awards.

Where to find me

Before you close this workbook, I would love to remind you that I am a real person who genuinely wants to support people on their healing journey. If you want to work with me, or just want to get in touch, you can contact me through my website or on social media.

Website: www.staceywebb.com.au
Facebook: facebook.com/StaceyWebbEFT
Instagram: instagram.com/_staceywebb
Amazon: amazon.com/author/staceywebb
Goodreads: goodreads.com/author/show/22384693.Stacey_Webb
TikTok: tiktok.com/@_staceywebb
Youtube: youtube.com/@Staceywebb

www.ingramcontent.com/pod-product-compliance
Lightning Source LLC
Chambersburg PA
CBHW050307010526
44107CB00055B/2140